W9-BKE-027

MEXICO CITY

TEXT: **M. WIESENTHAL**

Travesera de Gracia, 15 - Barcelona (21) - Spain

1st. Edition, July 1978
I.S.B.N.
84-7424-019-0

Library of Congress Catalog Card Number: 78-63020

This edition is published by Crescent Books, a division of Crown Publishers, Inc.

a b c d e f g h

CRESCENT BOOKS
New York

Mexico City is situated at 2,240 metres above sea level, between two mountain ranges covered with thick woods. It is, without any doubt, one of the most dynamic and densely populated cities in the whole American continent. But, it is above all else, a marvellous compendium of the Mexican soul; it is lively and bustling with its avenues and modern districts, sweet and poetic in its more intimate aspects, haughty in its gestures, generous in its gifts, valiant in its defiance, sentimental in its reminiscences...
When the first Spanish chronicler reached Tenochtitlan, the ancient Aztec capital, together with Hernàn Cortés, he described the amazement felt by the Spaniards on contemplating that prodigious city: "there were soldiers among us who had been in many parts of the world, in Constantinople, in the whole of Italy and Rome, and they said they had never seen a place so well encompassed, so harmonious and large and filled with so many people".
Thus was Tenochtitlan, the sacred city of an artistic and warlike people, the capital of an empire that covered almost all Mesoamerica.

Proud of itself
Tenochtitlan the city of Mexico arises.
Here no man fears death in war,
That is our glory.

The Great Temple of ancient Tenochtitlan (model).

This statue of the rain god, Tlaloc, is from Coatlinchán. It belongs to the Teotihuacán culture, to the classical period dating between 400 and 600 A.D.

Portrayals of family scenes are often found in the western region of Mexico.

Sorcerers played an important part in this society as they cured people and took part in the leadership of the group.

A view of the Maya room. Toltec room.

The market at Tlatelolco was the largest and most important in the centre of Mexico; there, objects from all parts of Mesoamerica were exchanged and courts of justice were held.

The Square of the Three Cultures in Tlatelolco.

Shrine to Ehécatl in the Pino Suárez underground train station.

Remains of the Great Temple of Tenochtitlan.

Monument to the People.

Plaque commemorating the first meeting of Moctezuma and Hernán Cortés.

Monument to the last Aztec Emperor, Cuauhtemoc.

The ruins of Tenochtitlan lie today like some deeply buried mysterious heart under modern Mexico City. There in the depths of the lagoon sleeps the sacred city with its canals and bridges, palaces and markets, places of worship and terraces. The hidden presence of this history can be appreciated in every part of the capital. In Mexico the deep voice of the earth can be felt. And perhaps, because of this, the history of the city resounds tremendously like some mysterious tremour.
Tenochtitlan had one of the best planned city centres of all the American civilizations. The symbol of this city was the great temple (teocalli) which stood in the square surrounded by a wall. Around this enormous pyramid were placed, in geometrically ordered groups, the buildings of the capital. The whole structure of the city was based on a prodigious feat of engineering, with ceramic pipes to distribute water, dykes to contain the overflow of the lake, deposits for collecting waste and garbage...

The National Palace.

La Campana de Dolores *in the National Palace.*

TIERRA Y

◁ The Madero Revolution, *1910.*

Murals by Diego Rivera in the National Palace.
Great Tenochtitlan, *(late XV century).*

A beautiful Aztec legend tells of the founding of Mexico-Tenochtitlan. The god of war, Huitzilopochtli, appeared one day before his priest Quauhcoatl and spoke to him thus: "You will see the cactus tenochtli and an eagle that will gaily perch on it. There we will settle and rule... There will be our city Mexico-Tenochtitlan..." Trusting in the word of their god, the people began to walk until they reached a marshy area; on a small island they saw an eagle devouring a serpent. And there among the reeds and canes, they founded their capital. The eagle, the serpent, and the cactus appear as a reference to this poetic legend, on the coat of arms of Mexico.

Seat of the Federal District Department (Town Hall).

The Metropolitan Cathedral.

The Sagrarium.

The interior.

Inside the Cathedral.

The main façade of the Colegio de las Vizcaínas.

Colegio de las Vizcaínas, main courtyard with central fountain.

Our Lady of Aránzazu, *by Cristobal de Villalpando, a painting on show in the Colegio de las Vizcaínas.*

When Cortes reached the city it had a population of more than half a million inhabitants. The Spaniards arrived as conquerors, but it would be no exaggeration to say that it was they who were conquered by the mysterious beauty of the city. Bernal Díaz del Castillo spoke of "things never before seen nor dreamed of". Hernán Cortés noted that, in many aspects, it was superior to the great cities of Europe.
The Aztec civilization, based on a rigid social organization had enormous refinement, besides a good knowledge of agriculture astronomy and art, etc. However, all this world was to disappear in a mysterious manner with the shock of confrontation with European culture. Moctezuma and his men

were crushed before the advance of the Spaniards. The last emperor Cuauhtemec, heroically defended his capital, but Cortes attacked the city and entered as a conqueror, but what a sad victory was that over a heap of smouldering ruins.
The history of the Viceroyalty of New Spain and the rebuilding of the ruined capital began with the arrival of the Spaniards. The Viceregal Government from 1535 was accompanied by missionaries whose evangelical task was to spread Christianity through the land, and at the same time study its ancient dead culture. Mexico City once more became the administrative and spiritual centre of this enterprise. The city had a university in 1551 and became one of the most active cultural centres in the New World. The Viceroys promoted the building of great palaces and the city became changed under the impulse of humanistic culture. And the proof that this task was not fruitless — having been undertaken by a lively and intelligent people — is the way in which, centuries later, Mexico took up European revolutionary traditions and faced her former conquerors in a noble struggle for

High Cloister of the Merced Convent.

XVI century mural fresco, The Adoration of the Kings, *at Culhuacan.*

Detail of Culhuacan.

The cloister at Culhuacan.

Vaulted niche in the Plaza de Loreto.

The house of the Counts of San Mateo de Valparaiso, seat of the National Bank of Mexico.

Façade of the Colegio de San Ildefonso.

Courtyard in the Colegio de San Ildefonso.

Interiors of colonial style courtyards.

The Church of the Carmen Convent at San Angel.

The Square and Church of Santo Domingo.

The Churches of San Juan de Dios and la Santa Veracruz.

The Church La Profesa.

Portal of San Francisco.

Churubusco.

The Casa Chata at Tlalpan.

Chimalistac.

Chimalistac.

Santa Catalina.

The Holy Trinity, finished in 1667.

The Iturbide Palace.

Façade of the Antiguo Colegio de Cristo.

The Casa de los Azulejos in the calle de Madero.

The house of the Majorat of Guerrero.

The former Casa de Moneda, now the Museum of the Cultures.

The San Carlos Academy

One of the late XVI century houses in Jesus Maria y Corregidora.

La Santa.Inquisición. *Antigua Escuela de Medicina.*

The Minería Palace.

independence. Their first heroes Hidalgo and Morelos were executed, but finally, Iturbide proclaimed the birth of the independent state of Mexico.
The capital lived intensely through these turbulent and at times dramatic years of its national history: empires and republics came and went, conservatives and liberals, democracies and dictatorships. Mexico had an adventurous existence — the armies of Independence, those of the United States, and of the Emperor Maximilian occupied the city in the XIX century. Later on during the 1910 revolution the peasant masses, followers of Pancho Villa and Zapata entered the capital. But the city kept on growing and was unharmed and indeed renewed by all these commotions. New districts were built, new avenues opened up and cultural life became intensified...
Thus the grandiose image of present day Mexico gradually began to take shape, like the body of an athlete that derives its strength from a fecund mixture of different blood and different cultures. From the Aztec pyramid to the skyscraper, a lot of history has unfolded, but the city has always remained faithful to its past and to its future, to its roots and its ideals, sunk into the earth like the cactus and the serpent, and flying high in the air like the eagle.

Inside a courtyard.

DAVID

A flower seller on one of the canals at Xochimilco.

THE MEXICAN PEOPLE

The traveller who arrives in our capital of course comes ready to enjoy the intoxicating atmosphere of a modern city to the full, and even knows the names of the main archaeological sites, and plans to visit all the museums and churches.
Mexico City is not going to disappoint him as it is so full of contrasts, but its real treasure is the people who live there. The privileged heir of a mixture of races and cultures, the Mexican has a marked personality. He loves dancing, singing, flowers, beauty and colour. Nevertheless he is externally rather taciturn as if he were afraid to give way to the expression of his soul. He does not conceive of life without honour, and his philosophy could be summed up in the verses of the Spanish classical poet:

Typical itinerant traders on the canals at Xochimilco

Visitors and Poncho sellers at Xochimilco..

Mariachis playing their trade.

Another view of a canal at Xochimilco.

The Grand Canal at Xochimilco.

That bright freedom
that where it found an honourable death
never wished to have a longer life.

Like all people from old countries, the Mexican has a deep sense of the meaning of life and is able to judge the human worth of his guests; he is highly sensitive to all the nuances of manners and mutual respect.
The Mexican practises what is almost a cult of hospitality. He always receives his guests with an embrace and is a master of the art of courtesy. A guest always feels completely at home and the common phrase "make yourself at home" has a deep significance as it allows us to get to know how a person who seems so polite really behaves in his daily private life.

THE CITY

Mexico is a city of contrasts. The natural forces of life have made it unique and beyond classification. Our capital is not like these old walled cities where everything is distributed according to its period or even according to strict social barriers. In Mexico everything is intermingled, —the oldest district with the most modern skyscraper, the purest baroque style church, with the most varied and noisy popular market. In some parts, the city has

The Chapultepec Woods.

preserved its colonial personality, with those red stone (tezontle) buildings that were so much admired by baron Humboldt. In many of the city's parks, the age-old mystery of the Aztec city hovering over the waters of the lake can still be felt. In the modern buildings of the University City, the rhythm of life is that of a great American metropolis. But there is also a style we could call Mexican, born of a wise mingling of cultures which has given its loveliest and most elegant creations to the Iturbide Palace and is seen in the buildings of the Colegio de Estudios and the Inquisicion. Apparently, our capital is not a well ordered city and it seems difficult to find one's way about, but let's not be put off by appearances. Things that are

The Chapultepec Woods.

For the person living in the capital, the old Chapultepec Woods are a great place for all kinds of entertainment and recreation.

The Zoological Gardens in Chapultepec.

The Castle of Chapultepec.

The Castle of Chapultepec (hill or mountain of the Chapulin *or* Grasshopper).

orderly on the outside and placed geometrically sometimes belie their appearance. And when one gets to know Mexico well, one is then able to understand its peculiar sense of order. Life and history have developed the image of this city in a natural, almost intuitive way. And finally everything has remained in its right place. Even the emigrants here form groups according to their nationality and constitute genuine guilds of commercial specialities; — the Spaniards are the restauranteurs and grocers, the French are in charge of the textile factories and department stores, the Germans are in the coffee plantations, and the English in the most modern industries.

The streets are grouped in a similar way according to their specialities. In the calle de Donceles are the furniture shops, in the calle de Tacuba, shoe shops, in the calle de Madero, luxurious shops selling imported goods.
The life of the city is centred round those districts that absorb the vast waves of traffic and trade; — the Avenida Madero, the Avenida Juárez and the Paso de la Reforma...
The key point of reference never to be forgotten for getting one's bearings in our capital is the Avenida de los Insurgentes which crosses the city from north to south, from the Carretera de Laredo to the University City.

The National History Museum in the Castle of Chapultepec.

State coach belonging to the Emperor Maximilian.

The carriage of the Benemérito Licenciado Don Benito Juárez.

The shape and elevation of Mexico City, *a map by Gomez de Trasmonte in 1628.*

An XVIII painting depicting the Baptism of a local chief.

The Standard of the Conquest, *a XVI century oil painting.*

Forma y Levantado de la Ciudad de Mexico.
Por la correspondencia de los numeros se Señalan En Esta Copia los conventos y cosas señalados.
A. Palacio Rl.
B. Cathedral.
C. Casa de Cabildo.
D. Casa Arpl.
F. Uniuersidad.
G. Alameda.

TE ESTANDAR-TE EL FUE EL QUE TRAJO Dn. FER-NAN-DO COR-TE

The Chamber of Independence, a mural fresco by Juan O'Gorman, 1961.

Juárez and Reform, *a mural fresco by José Clemente Orozco, 1948.*

Equestrian portrait of the Emperor Maximilian.

Equestrian portrait of Porfirio Diaz. *An oil painting by the Catalan painter J. Cusachs. 1901.*

The traveller must also get used to vast dimensions. But at the same time he must not miss the infinite details that are so easily hidden among so much bustle and animation. Some parts of the Avenida Madero still preserve the romantic atmosphere of that elegant capital of the twenties with its frenchified air. In the Paseo de la Reforma, the styles of modern Mexico are mingled with reminiscences of the period of the Emperor Maximilian. Not forgetting the poetic atmosphere of the tiny streets of old Mexico; the colonial houses of the calle Donceles, the porticoes of the Plaza de Santo Domingo... etc. A living example of this mixture of styles is to be found in the square of Las Tres Culturas, where all periods of Mexican history converge.

EL ZOCALO

The Plaza de la Constitución, popularly known as el Zocalo, is the city centre. The great avenues of Madero, 5 de Mayo, and 16 de Septiembre open out onto its spacious geometrical vastness. Around it are also the main civil and religious monuments of Mexico — the cathedral, the Palacio Nacional and the Supreme Court of Justice.
In the centre of the square there should have been a

BATALLON
SUPREMOS PODERES
57

Detail from the semicircular monument to Juárez.

monument to Independence, but the Spanish architect Lorenzo de la Hidalga who was commissioned to build it in 1843 only managed to construct the plinth, which is the origin of the popular name of the square.
This is the place where all the excitement is to be found during the most important events in the Mexican calender — September 15th when the Noche del Grito (the Night of the Shout) is celebrated to commemorate the proclamation of Independence, the 1st of May — Labour Day, November 20th, the anniversary of the 1910 revolution.
On the Noche del Grito we commemorate the proclamation of Independence made on September 15th 1810 by the priest Miguel Hidalgo y Castilla. The old bell the priest had rung to call the people to rebellion has been installed in the Palacio Nacional.
The Noche del Grito is always celebrated amid exuberant popular jubilation. The square is filled with an excited crowd awaiting the peal of bells and the President's traditional "shout" from the palace balcony.
The most characteristic monument in el Zocalo is, without any doubt, the Metropolitan Cathedral, a fine church whose construction was begun in the XVI century. Its towers were designed by the XVIII century Mexican architect José Damián Ortiz de Castro who thought of the unusual finishing touch on the top —two volcanic stone bells from Tezontle faced with chiluca.
The interior of the cathedral is a prodigy of the baroque. The altar of the kings, occupying the cathedral apse is, in itself, a masterpiece of metal work. The artist Jerónimo de Balbas took ten years to make it.
Another outstanding work is the choir surrounded by a rail made of a mixture of gold, copper, and silver made in China. The ivory and fine wood lectern is an exquisite Philippine work of art dating from the XVIII century. Next to the cathedral is the Metropolitan Sagrarium built in the XVIII century, whose portals are a masterpiece of the churrigueresque baroque style.
The Palacio Nacional occupies all the eastern side of the Plaza de la Constitución. This used to be the property of the descendents of Cortes until the Spanish monarchs made it the Viceregal residence. All the upper part of the building was added in 1927 to give the facade a better line and make it more impressive. In the niche on the main door is the bell which the priest Hidalgo used to call the people together during the Independence rebellion. Inside the palace are kept the famous paintings and murals by Diego Rivera that reconstruct all the history of Mexico, from Quetzalcoatl, the civilizing god of the Toltecs, to the revolutionary caudillos. In other murals, Rivera gives us an idea of the old capital of Tenochtitlan and the arts and crops of prehispanic Mexico. On the lower floor of the palace is the Archivo General de la Nación (General national archives) where valuable historical documents are kept showing the different constitutions the country has had. In another wing of the building is the Juarez Museum where there are collected many souvenirs of that president.
Also in the Plaza del Zócalo is the Supreme Court of Justice built in 1940 and decorated inside with magnificent paintings by José Clemente Crozco and the North American George Biddle.

An urban view of the Federal District of Mexico.

THE CHURCHES OF MEXICO

The history of the capital is closely linked to the work of the religious orders. From the earliest times of the conquest the following orders arrived in Mexico and spread their convents and foundations throughout the country — the Franciscans (1524), Dominicans (1526) Augustinians (1533), and the Jesuits in 1572.
The first Viceroy Antonio de Mendoza unified the building of convents. Their construction generally consisted of three sections, — the walled atrium, the church, and the convent itself with its cloister. The religious buildings were in many cases more luxurious than the civil ones. The traveller will find them in different parts of the city mainly grouped in the older districts. Some of them are so large that today they are able to house several buildings. The convent of la Enseñanza for example now houses the Palace of Justice and the Colegio Nacional... The convent of Santa Catalina de Siena houses the School of Jurisprudence, a barracks and several homes. Other religious residences such as San Pablo were converted into hospitals; some, like San Augustin and las Betlemitas were made into libraries and others such as Santa Clara into flats and offices.
After the Reform in 1857 with the nationalization of church property, many convents were demolished to give way to the construction of the city and to facilitate communication. In only one night, President Juárez ordered the demolition of the church of San Andrés where the body of the Emperor Maximilian had lain.

From all this religious past, the only churches remaining today are the baroque San Lorenzo, La Encarnación, Santiago Tlatelolce, Santa Teresa the Ancient, La Profesora, etc. Not forgetting the most important churrigueresque style churches of El Sagrario, La Santísima Trinidad, La Santa Veracruz, San Francisco and La Enseñanza.

THE MODERN CITY

The demolition of the old convents was a positive step to the modernization of the city. Nevertheless the most important urban enterprise of the XIX century was the opening up of what is now the Paseo de la Reforma, instigated in 1864 by the Emperor Maximilian. This avenue, communicating the old city with the peaceful Chapultepec woods where the emperors resided, favoured the growth of the city towards the west. Along this avenue with its beautiful statues and summer houses, are the great buildings of Mexico's modern architecture.

Semicircular monument to Don Benito Juárez.

Monument to the Revolution.

The city's present day north-south axis is made up of the Avenida de los Insurgentes which crosses the Paseo de la Reforma at the statue of Cuauhtemoc and leads to the University City.
The rapid growth of the city and its population during the last quarter century has given rise to many transport and housing problems. New roads have been built to solve these difficulties, — Tlalpan, Viaducto Miguel Alemán, the Anillo Periférico (ring road), and a network of suburban underground trains. To solve the housing problem satellite cities have been built on the outskirts. Tlatelolce city, situated in the northern area of the capital brings together the whole of the history of

Monument to the Boy Heroes.

Monument to the Mother. ▷

Mexico in the Square of the three Cultures (la Plaza de las Tres Culturas) : these are, the prehispanic culture seen in the remains of the pyramid; the viceregal culture exemplified by the church of Santa Cruz de Tlatelolce where Fray Bernardino de Sahagun taught, and the modern culture with its skyscrapers and magnificent Foreign Affairs Ministery building.

One of the grandest examples of Mexico's modern architecture is the university city, built in volcanic rock on prehispanic pyramidical forms. The city can hold a student population of 100,000 students and is considered one of the foremost intellectual centres of South America.

The Caballito *pavilion and the new National Lottery building.*

Equestrian statue of Carlos IV, called El Caballito, *by Tolsa.*

The Columbus pavilion in the Paseo de la Reforma.

Monument to Columbus.

EL AHORRO NACIONAL
CON FUTURO

Monument to the foundation of Mexico City.

A view of the calle de Florencia in the so-called "Pink Zone".

The Monument to Independence. "El Angel".

PLAZA

The Theatre of the Insurgents – a mosaic mural by Diego Rivera.

The Post Office.

Hotels and buildings in modern Mexico.

The monument to the oil industry.

The University City. The Library with its wall mosaics by Juan O'Gorman, depicting different phases of the history of Mexico.

Poliforum cultural Siqueiros.

The Mall, *a mural painting by Diego Rivera.*

A night-time view of the Avenida Juárez.

The Latinamerican Tower with its 44 storys taken from the Central Mall.

SEGUROS
6:57 53
LATINOAMERICANA

The Modern Art Museum.

THE MUSEUMS

Mexico is one of the most important world centres for archaeological studies. In its Anthropology and Historical Institute are specialists of every nationality, but it is sufficient to visit the National Anthropological Museum to see the infinite riches that history has left behind in the earth of this country. More than one museum could be said to be an authentic house of culture conceived with a deep sense of devotion to learning, for visitors to understand the value of these pieces of prehispanic art. The first rooms in the museum introduce us to the initial phases of the mesoamerican cultures, from the early emigrants who crossed the Behring Strait. This was fundamentally a farming culture as they were aware of all the secrets of plant cultivation. Then came the fabulous but cruel culture of Teotihuacan, — the city of great pyramids and temples. Teotihuacan means "the place where the gods were created" and is the sanctuary of Mesoamerican mythology. We also find impressive works in stone sculpted by Toltec warriors and a central room devoted to their most brilliant successors, the Mexics or Aztecs. The Mexican room is dominated by the famous circular earth calender weighing twenty-four tons, which was built in the reign of Moctezuma. Here are all the remains of this dreamlike melancholy culture that witnessed the arrival of Cortes and his soldiers with a tired, sceptical and knowing air.
The entire history of the mesoamerican peoples is to be found in the Anthropological Museum — the Oaxaca civilizations, the Gulf cultures, the mathematical and magical wisdom of the Mayas. The museum is situated in the Chapultepec woods on a wide esplanade overlooked by the statue of the rain god Tlaloc. It has a library with more than 100,000 volumes and is the seat of the National School of Anthropology.

THE COLONIAL RELIGIOUS ART MUSEUM

Installed in the former convent of San Diego, a baroque building dating from the first half of the XVIII century, is a collection of the most representative works of Mexican painting from the colonial period, dating from 1521 to 1821.
The majority of the works on show in the Viceregal Art Gallery in San Diego are from the original collections of the San Carlos Museum.

THE MODERN ART MUSEUM

Situated at the entrance to the Chapultepec woods, the Modern Art Museum was inaugurated in 1964. One of its rooms is devoted to the works of the great landscape artist José María Velasco, and in another room are the works of the great Mexican masters of contemporary painting — Doctor Alt, José Clemente Orozco, Diego Rivera, Alfaro Siqueiros, and Rufino Tamayo.

THE NATIONAL HISTORY MUSEUM

This collection is kept in Chapultepec castle. On its two storys is the whole history of Mexico, — before the conquest, the period of the conquest, Mexico City, the Viceroyalty, Independence, the Porfiriato, and the Revolution. A visit to this museum allows us to see the state rooms of the castle where the Emperor Maximilian and several later presidents resided.

Views of the Modern Art Museum.

The Fine Arts Palace.

"Man in the time machine" a mural by Diego Rivera in the Fine Arts Palace.

A mural by the painter Rufino Tamayo, Mexico Today, *1952, in the Fine Arts Palace.*

A mural by Jorge González Camarena, Humanity frees itself from Misery, *1960.*

Courtyard of the San Carlos Museum.

A room in the San Carlos Museum.

The Palace of the counts of Santiago de Calimaya, now the City Museum.

Gargoyles in the shape of cannon.

The National Museum of Arts and Popular Industries..

The Fountain of the Guitar-Playing Mermaid.

Foot of the staircase.

MUSEO NACIONAL DE ARTES
E INDUSTRIAS POPULARES

PINACOTECA
VIRREINAL
PINTURA SIGLOS XVI XVII XVIII
INBAL
SEP

Views of the San Diego Viceregal art collection.

Details of the interior of the San Diego Viceregal art collection.

The Charrería Museum.

A Charro chair.

A Charro hat.

A room in the Charrería Museum.

THE POPULAR ARTS MUSEUM

Those fond of craft work must see the magnificent collections kept in this museum which was formerly the convent of Corpus Cristi. Only the small church has survived from the old building where noble indian girls, the daughters of local landowners took their vows.

CHAPULTEPEC

The Chapultepec woods, situated in an idyllic spot full of evocative historical reminiscences, is the most popular place for a walk in the whole of Mexico city. The Aztec kings left their statues sculpted in the stones in the park. The old Tenochticlan kings built a palace there that sadly contemplated its own reflection in the waters of a lake surrounded by weeping willows. For many years it provided the water supply for the city by means of a prodigious system of pipes and aqueducts. The Military College used to be in the castle and it was heroically defended by its

Dancing masks.

Polychromed pottery from Metepec, State of Mexico.

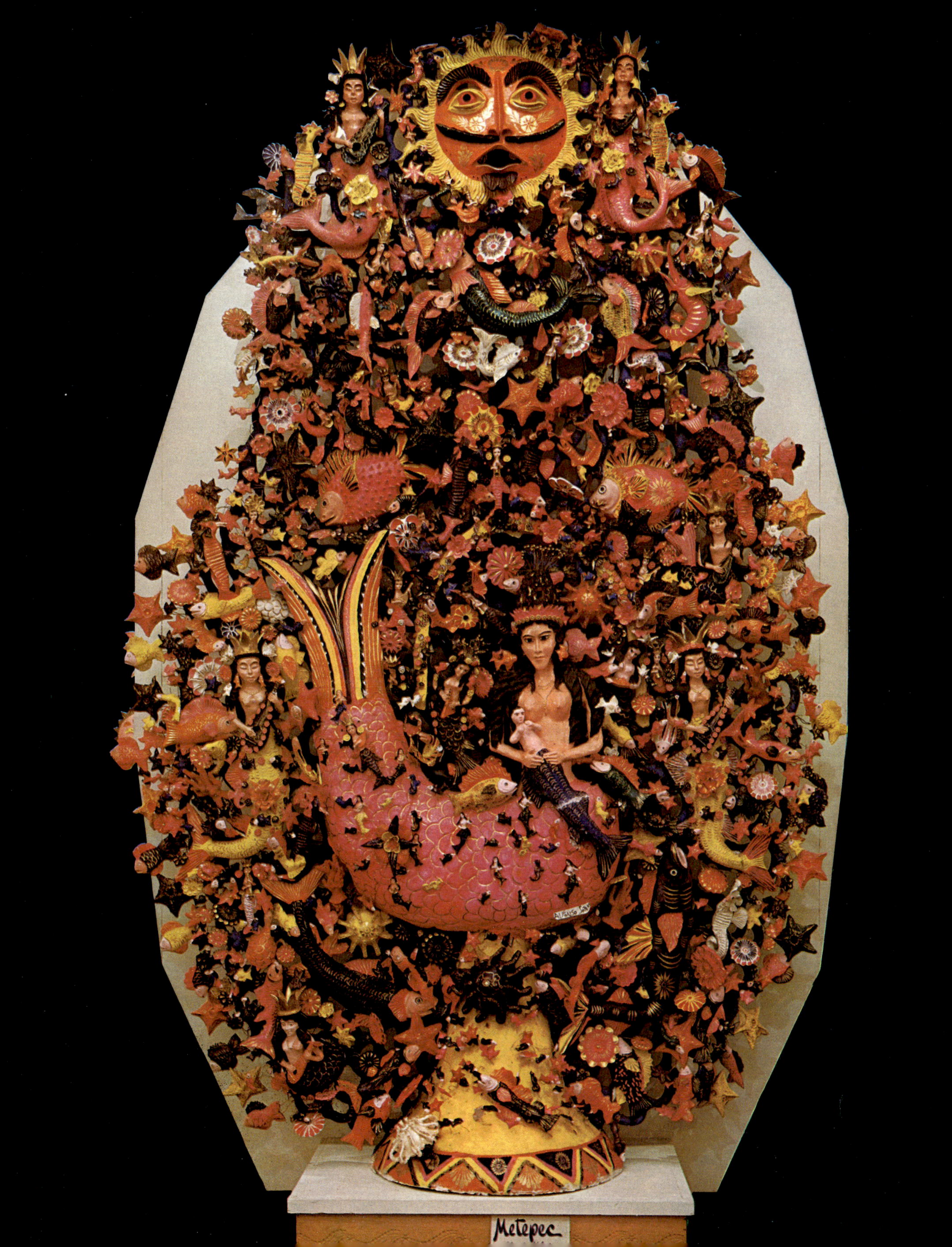
Metepec

students in 1847 against the soldiers of North America. At the entrance to the wood a monument to the Boy Heroes has been built to commemorate their bravery.
In Chapultepec, nature and art, history and the everyday life of the city blend together in perfect harmony. The passers-by saunter round the statues and monuments in search of peacefulness in the lakes and woods. Picnic areas, fun fairs, and zoos exist side by side with great museums and history-laden stones.
It is said that the Aztecs planted the giant ahuehuete trees that shade the park. There are more than 200 trees of this species, imported from North America, in this wood. The largest of all, Moctezuma's ahuehuete, is fifteen metres in circumference and more than forty metres high. The wood has been extended to the southeast to

Handwork from the whole of the Mexican Republic.

The sale of typical candles in the "Pink Zone".

Mexican paper flowers.

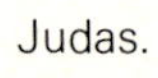

Judas.

Handicrafts; the corner of a shop.

Lacas.

Piñatas.

A Charro hat seller.

The garden of Art.

The la Lagunilla Market.

A portrait artist in wax in the garden of Art.

include a Natural History Museum, an artificial lake, and El Lago, one of the Capital's most luxurious restaurants.

THE FLOATING GARDENS OF XOCHIMILCO

The Aztecs built their capital of palaces and pyramids amid decorative trees and gardens. Today the city has many green areas — Chapultepec, Popotla, Postal, San Lucas, San Cosme, etc. But of the famous floating gardens or "chinampas" that amazed the Spaniards when they reached the lake of Tenochtitlan, there only remains the gardens of Xochimilco. Every Sunday, Xochimilco welcomes a vast number of visitors who sail along its canals in flower-decked gondolas. Everything floats in Xochimilco, — the flower shops, restaurants, and

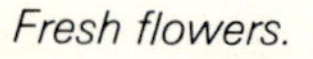

Fresh flowers.

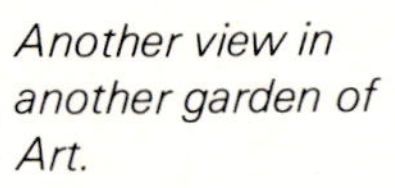

Another view in another garden of Art.

"Bazar del sábado", the fountain used as a gigantic fruit-dish.

Paintings on fig leaf paper.

Paintings on fig leaf paper and textiles.

Detail of a typical Mexican kitchen.

A kitchen in the Frida Khalo Museum at Coyoacán.

Stuffed chillis - Chilli gravy - Tacos - Cheesies - pancakes - fried beans - Salad made of alligator pear - chilli sauces.

picturesque "curios" selling souvenirs and nick-nacks.

THE MARKETS

The markets constitute one of the most picturesque sights in the life of Mexico city. They are living museums where the personality of the country is well represented. Silent indians practise the refined art of trading seated amid their wares, — pottery, flowers, hand-painted vegetable matting. Here, you can buy at a reasonable price all kinds of small objects created with the same ability and patience that the old Aztec masters put into their work.
The La Lagunilla and Tepito markets offer the traveller an incredible variety of antiques, old objects, and books. Not all the things on sale in these markets are guaranteed to be genuine. But from time to time a collector may find something of value.
Exquisite silverware can be bought at street markets, but perhaps it is more advisable to go to a specialized shop. Mexico is the most important silver producing country in the world and the country's craftsmen use this metal to create authentic masterpieces in the shape of rings, bracelets, necklaces, earrings, etc.

THE MARIACHIS OF THE PLAZA GARIBALDI

Although they do not constitute one of the

The Red Sun *by Alexander Calder, with the Aztec Stadium in the background.*

Stadium in the University City. Sports Palace.

The Enclosure, *a bronze over the entrance to the monumental Bull Ring by Alfredo Just.*

Charro Painting. The National Sport.

Scenes from a charreada. ▷

PORRA!
ASOCIACION DE CHARROS
EL HORMIGUERO

A folklore ballet in the Fine Arts Palace.

Xiuhcoatl (serpent) of Tenayuca (bordering the State of Mexico).

profounder aspects of Mexican life, the Mariachis — groups of guitar players and trumpeters dressed in regional costumes — are a pleasant tourist attraction. Their centre of operations is in the Plaza Garibaldi, around a famous tavern known as El Tenampa. The Mariachis are from the state of Jalisco and its capital Guadalajara, which is also the land of the "charros" and of so many songs which have become world famous.

THE CUISINE OF MEXICO

Mexican cuisine has developed like the history of the country, out of a rich intermingling. Here, the products of the soil of America are mixed with elements of Spanish cooking. World gastronomy is endebted, (a fact which is sometimes forgotten), to the New World, as many fruits and grains still conserve the nahuatl root of their names: — tomatoe, avocado pear, cocoa, cacahuete (peanut), and chocolate. Even the Mexican "chile" (chilli) is known in many countries as pimiento (pepper) because of Columbus' mistake in confusing its strong taste with that of pepper. The word tomatoe means "fatness". Chocolate (xocotl atl) means fruit water, as the Mexicans drank it diluted in water or sweetened with maguey honey.
The Spaniards, in their turn, contributed many products to Mexican cookery, — wheat, rice, sugar, oil, sheep, pigs, oranges, etc.
Maize is the basis of Mexican cookery, together with chilli which gives all their dishes that unmistakable picant flavour.
The most typical dish is without doubt the "mole poblano", which is a stew with turkey meat and pork cooked in a thick sauce of ground chillis with a little chocolate added.
The national drink is pulque, extracted from the "pita", which in Mexico is called magüey. This is a strong smelling drink which when distilled produces tequila and mezcal. Tequila is drunk according to the classic ritual of putting a little salt on one's tongue, biting a slice of lemon, and immediately swallowing a mouthful of the liquor.
Among the tastiest products of the land of Mexico, mention must be made, of course, of the extraordinary assortment of tropical fruit which makes an attractive and appetizing decoration for any table.

CRAFT WORK

The prolific baroque style imagination of the Mexican people is shown in their craft work. The Museum of Art and Popular Industries is responsible for promoting the many types of handicrafts developed in the different regions of the country, — pottery, wicker work, cloth, work in stone, glass, gold, silver, leather, etc.
The native pottery has an enormous variety of pieces and enjoys great prestige among the peasants who prefer their food to be prepared in earthenware bowls. The black pottery of Oaxaca is outstanding for its decorative qualities as are the polychromed pieces from Puebla. The decorative ware from Guanajuato, ochre in colour, is of a fine design.
The making of glass which was introduced by the Spaniards found some very good exponents in Mexico. At the present time there are very few glass making workshops in Mexico city, but their jars, miniatures and decorative objects are much appreciated by collectors.
The local hand-woven cloth industry produces a tremendous variety of cotton and woollen cloth. The cloth used for making the typical articles of clothing is made of cotton.
Fine wood carvings can be bought in the popular markets, and this is one of the most characteristic crafts of the indian creative genius. Wood carvers from rural areas still make crucifixes and images of saints.

The Tenayuca Pyramid.

With reeds, cane, bamboo, magüey and willow, the indians make a wide variety of things such as baskets, matting and trays.
Native artisanry is also outstanding in fine metal work including gold. In specialized shops there is wonderful filigree work done in the old pre-columbian tradition.

THE OUTSKIRTS OF MEXICO CITY

Many of the historic towns surrounding Mexico City have been integrated into the confines of the Federal District, and are linked to the city by a rapid communication service.

TLALPAN

In this quiet wooded town, which was a summer resort of the Viceroys, the atmosphere, redolent of the colonial period, has been preserved. Its "spouting fountains" surrounded by old trees and its streets winding among the archards and gardens of great aristocratic mansions, are one of the favourite excursions people take. Some of its historical houses have been preserved.

CHURUBUSCO

An ancient Aztec sanctuary with a fine viceregal art museum installed in the old convent of St. Thomas.

COYOACAN

This was the headquarters of Hernán Cortés while the capital Tenochtitlan was being rebuilt. It was here where the Conquistador founded the first Town Hall. Cortes' palace, rebuilt and moved from its original location can still be visited in the main square of the town. Coyoacan has also preserved some lovely colonial style houses and also some churches and convents.

Wall with serpents.

Double staircase on the Tenayuca Pyramid.

Detail from the serpents footstool.

A colonial corner in Culhuacan.

Colonial view at Coyoacán.

CALLE
CALLE
TRES
CRUCES
Z.P.21

Another pilgrimage bearing the Homeland Standard.

The New Basílica of Our Lady of Guadalupe.

The Old Basílica.

Pilgrimages in the province, on the way to the Basílica of Guadalupe.

SAN ANGEL

This is one of the most picturesque towns in the Federal District and one of those that has best preserved the memory of the colonial period. A museum of Colonial art has been installed in the old convent of el Carmen, a building of great architectural beauty.

THE GARDEN CITIES OF EL PEDREGAL AND SAN JERONIMO

During the last few years modern residential colonies and large country houses have been built in this area of the Federal District. The Mexican Institute of Social Security has created a satellite city — la Unidad Independencia — composed of apartments which are surrounded by gardens.

SAN JUAN DE ARAGON, MIXCOAC AND TACUBAYA

In these villages, which in the XIX century made up the peasant belt of Mexico city, residential districts, and urban development areas with popular housing have been constructed.

TACUBA

Sited on one of the most important roads of old Tenochtitlan, the town still preserves its fine Franciscan church and plateresque doorway. On the Mexico City — Tacuba road, surrounded by a railing, is the tree at which, according to legend, Cortes stopped to lament his defeat on the Noche Triste (sad night) of June 30th 1520.

AZCAPOTZALCO

The ancient capital of the Tepaneca Empire, it has preserved a Dominican convent dating from the colonial period. But its long history has had to give way to the modern industrial development of the region. Refineries and factories have given a definitive burial to the town's archaeological past.

GUADALUPE

The town of Guadalupe Hidalgo is situated to the north of Mexico City, in an area that was formerly inhabited by the Aztecs. But the essential part of Guadalupe is its basilica, the church where the Black Virgin, Patroness of the Mexican nation, is worshipped.

The Mexican Virgin of Guadalupe has an interesting legend. On December 12th 1531, the Virgin appeared to the shepherd Juan Diego, a converted indian. The Virgin asked him to pick a small bunch of flowers from the hillside, and put them in his cloak and show them to the bishop. Juan Diego did this, and when he opened his cloak to show the flowers, the image of the Virgin was found to be imprinted in the cloth. The bishop kept the miraculous cloak and ordered a sanctuary to be built where the image could be worshipped.

Since that time, devotion to the Virgin of Guadalupe has taken root in the soul of the Mexican people. Even the colonial Spaniards, perhaps in memory of the Virgin of Guadalupe worshipped in Extremadura, immediately identified themselves with this deeply spontaneous sentiment. The Virgin born from the earth, appearing like springtime among the flowers — an indian, and dark-skinned — she gave a feminine soul to the virile and warlike lands of the conquest. Thousands of pilgrims visit the shrine at all times of the year, and especially during the festivities on December 12th to worship their Patroness. She is the symbol of the hopes of the people, and it was not in vain that the priest Hidalgo had her image put on the flag of rebellion. The church has been restored on many occasions through the centuries. But the whole of it, from its towers to the sagrarium, exudes the tense and mysterious atmosphere of the miracle. It is here, in Guadalupe, where the image of the Mexican people is seen in its most beautiful, generous, and hopeful light.

Façade of the Basílica.

Chapel of the Cerrito in La Villa.

Chapel of the Pocito in La Villa. ▷

The New Basílica of the Virgin of Guadalupe.

INDEX